Ukulele *from the* Beginning

Songbook

Published by
Chester Music Limited
14-15 Berners Street,
London W1T 3LJ, UK.

Exclusive Distributors:
Music Sales Limited
Distribution Centre, Newmarket Road,
Bury St Edmunds, Suffolk IP33 3YB, UK.

Music Sales Corporation
257 Park Avenue South, New York, NY10010
United States of America.

Music Sales Pty Limited
20 Resolution Drive,
Caringbah, NSW 2229, Australia.

Book content and layout by Camden Music.
Compiled by Christopher Hussey.
Edited by Rachel Payne.

Printed in the EU.

www.musicsales.com

About the book

This book is the ideal repertoire for one of today's most popular instruments. Versatile and adaptable, the ukulele has been around since the late 19th century and is now enjoying a remarkable surge of popularity. It's inexpensive, easy to learn and suitable for all ages.

This book presents a great collection of simple songs which use only the chords taught in *Ukulele from the Beginning Book 1*. This makes it ideal extra repertoire for those following the course, and a perfect beginner songbook in itself. Chord diagrams and strumming suggestions are indicated at the top of every page.

The ukulele is a great place to start enjoying music in the classroom and this book makes the process a pleasure for teacher and children alike.

Contents

Bobby Shafto

Bob - by Shaf - to's gone to sea,___ sil - ver buck - les on his knee;___

he'll come back and mar - ry me,___ bon - ny Bob - by Shaf - to.

Bob - by Shaf - to's bright and fair, comb - ing down his yel - low hair;

he's my own for ev - er - more, bon - ny Bob - by Shaf - to.

Swing Low, Sweet Chariot

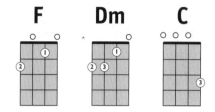

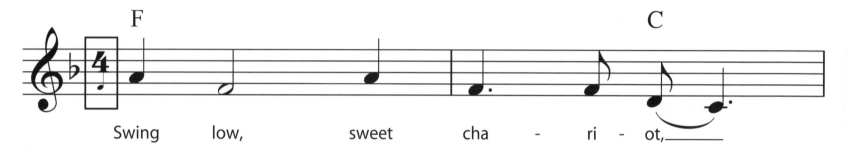

Swing low, sweet cha - ri - ot,____

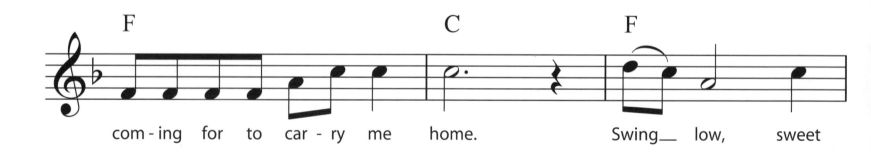

com - ing for to car - ry me home. Swing__ low, sweet

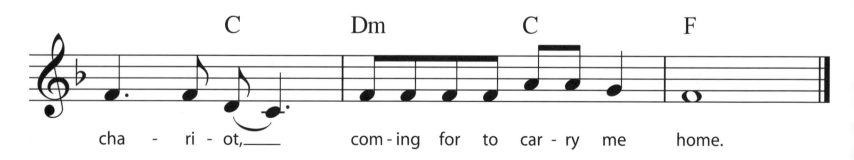

cha - ri - ot,____ com - ing for to car - ry me home.

Amazing Grace

Early One Morning

Ear - ly one mor - ning, just as the sun was ri - sing, I

heard a maid - en sing - ing in the val - ley be - low:

"Oh, don't de - ceive___ me, oh, nev - er leave___ me!

How___ could you use___ a___ poor___ maid - en so?"

Away In A Manger

A - way   in   a___   man - ger,   no___   crib   for   a

bed,   the___   lit - tle   Lord   Je - sus   laid___   down   His   sweet

head.   The   stars   in   the___   bright   sky   looked___   down   where   He

lay,   the___   lit - tle   Lord   Je - sus   a - sleep   on   the   hay.

The Skye Boat Song

Speed bon - ny boat, like a bird on the wing,

'on - ward', the sail - ors cry._____

Car - ry the lad that's born to be king

o - ver the sea to Skye._____

Merrily We Roll Along

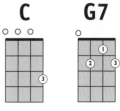

Mer - ri - ly we roll a - long, roll a - long, roll a - long.

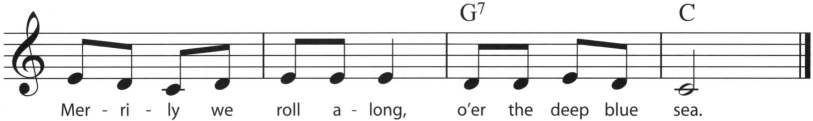

Mer - ri - ly we roll a - long, o'er the deep blue sea.

The Keel Row

N.B. The '&'s should be swung.

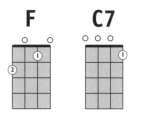

Swung

As I came through Sand - gate, through Sand - gate, through

A-tisket, A-tasket

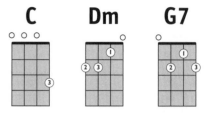

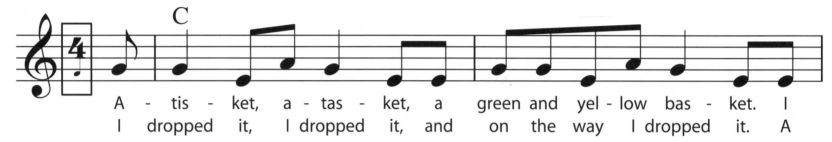

A - tis - ket, a - tas - ket, a   green and yel - low bas - ket. I
I dropped it, I dropped it, and   on the way I dropped it. A

wrote a let - ter to my love and   on the way I dropped it.
lit - tle girl - ie picked it up and   put it in her pock - et.

Silent Night

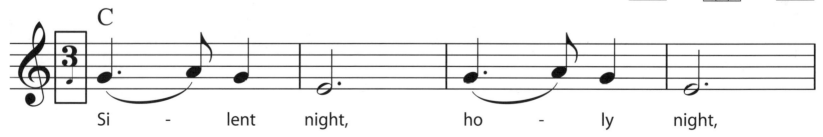

Si - lent night,   ho - ly night,

Twinkle, Twinkle, Little Star

Yankee Doodle

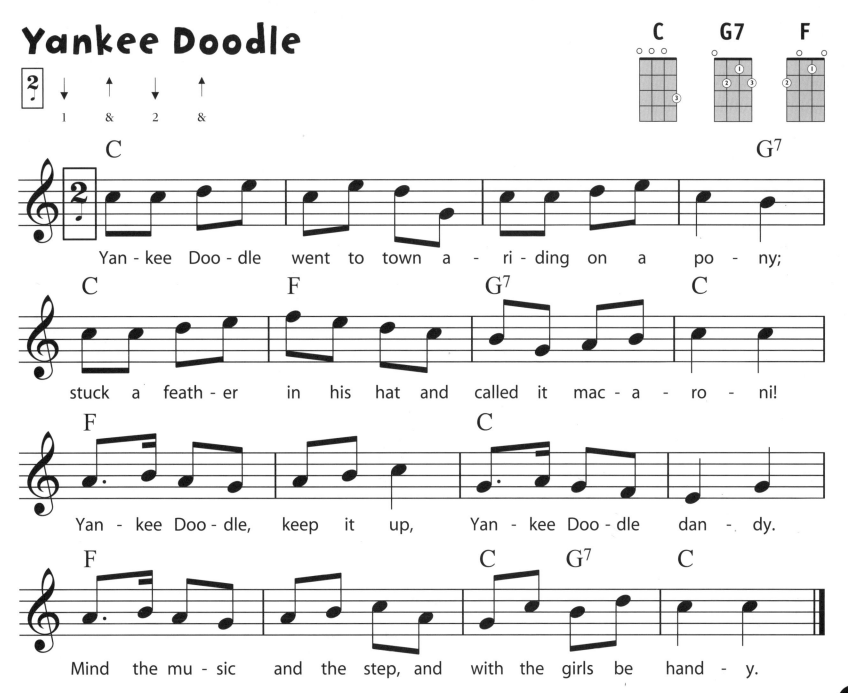

Summer Is Icumen In

Home On The Range

Deck The Halls

Yule - tide car - ol, fa la la la la, la la la la.

Scarborough Fair

Are you go - ing to Scar - bor - ough Fair? Par - sley,

sage, rose - mar - y and thyme. Re - mem - ber me to

one who lives there,___ she once was a true love of mine.

The Yellow Rose Of Texas

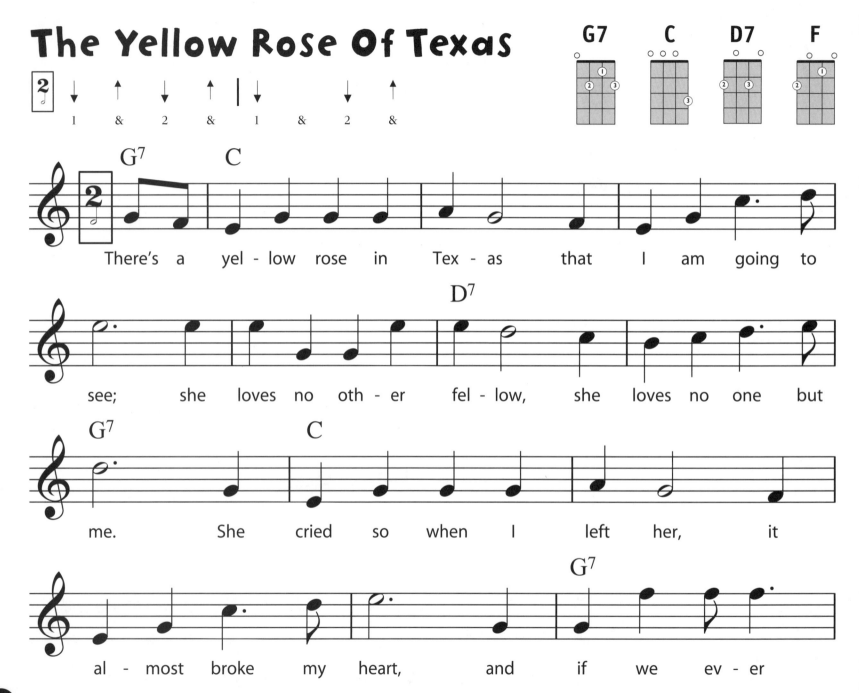

meet a - gain, we nev - er more will part.

Michael Finnegan

There was an old man called Mi - chael Fin - ne - gan,

he grew whis - kers on his chin - e - gan, the wind came up and

blew them in a - gain, poor old Mi - chael Fin - ne - gan, be - gin a - gain...

Danny Boy

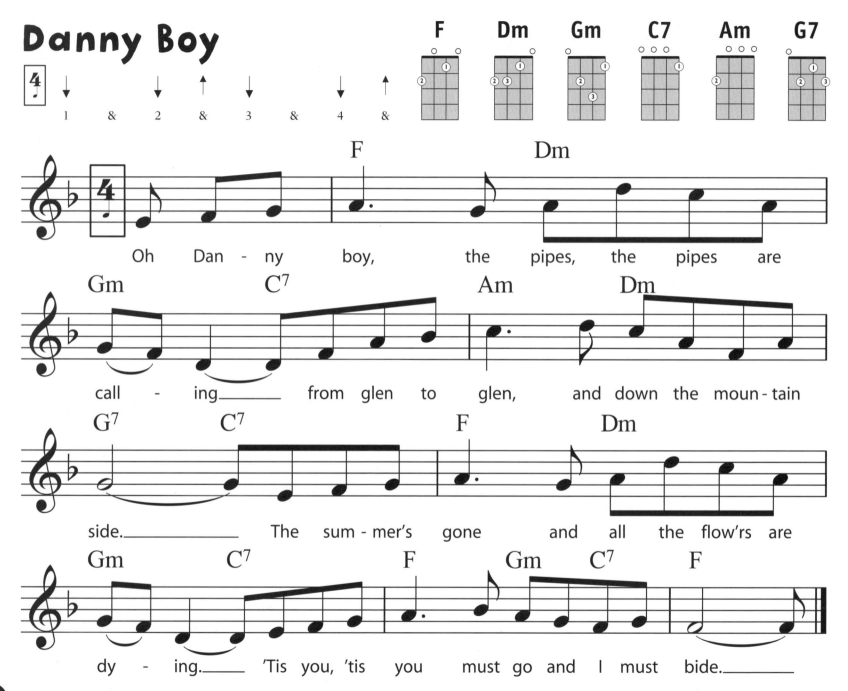

On Top Of Old Smokey

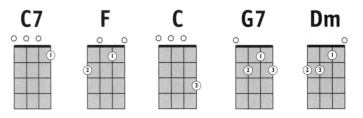

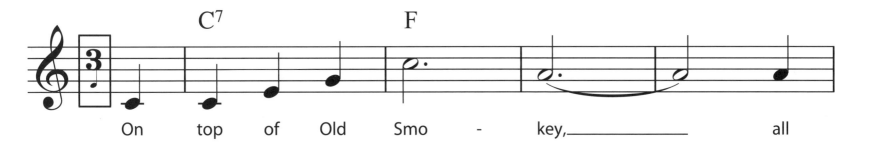

On   top   of   Old   Smo   -   key,_____   all

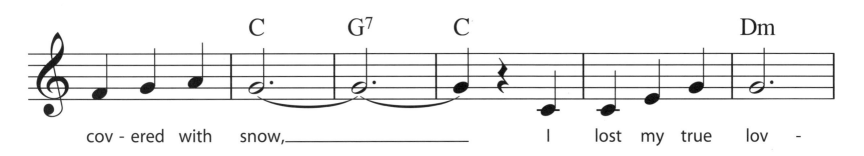

cov - ered   with   snow,_____   I   lost   my   true   lov -

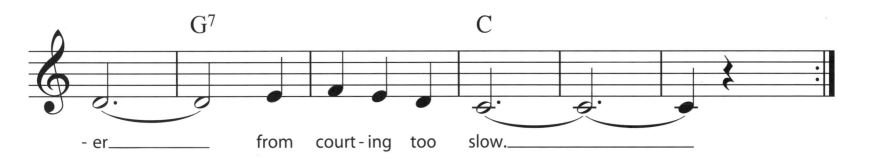

- er_____   from   court - ing   too   slow._____

Kalinka

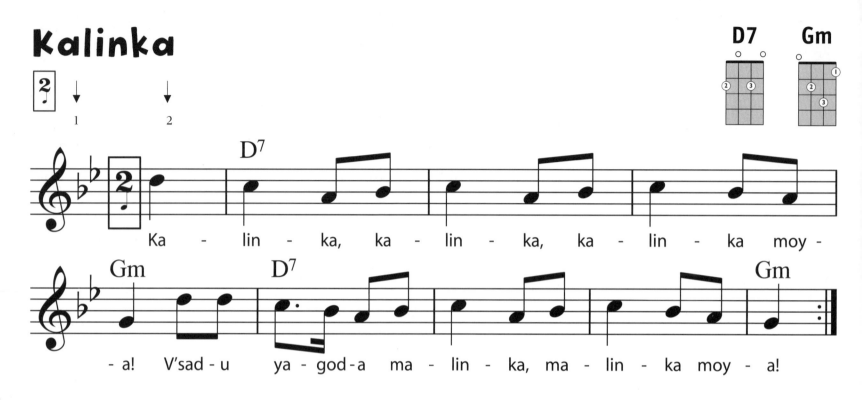

Ka - lin - ka, ka - lin - ka, ka - lin - ka moy - a! V'sad - u ya - god - a ma - lin - ka, ma - lin - ka moy - a!

Joshua Fought The Battle Of Jericho

N.B. The '&'s should be swung.

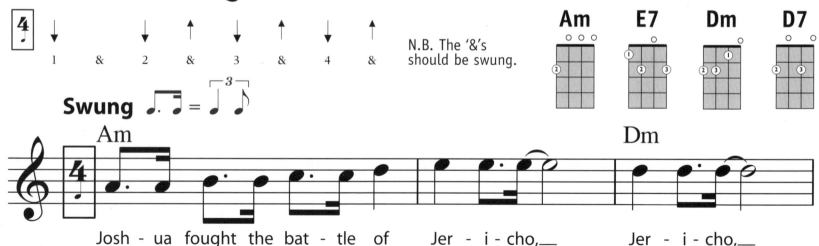

Josh - ua fought the bat - tle of Jer - i - cho,__ Jer - i - cho,__

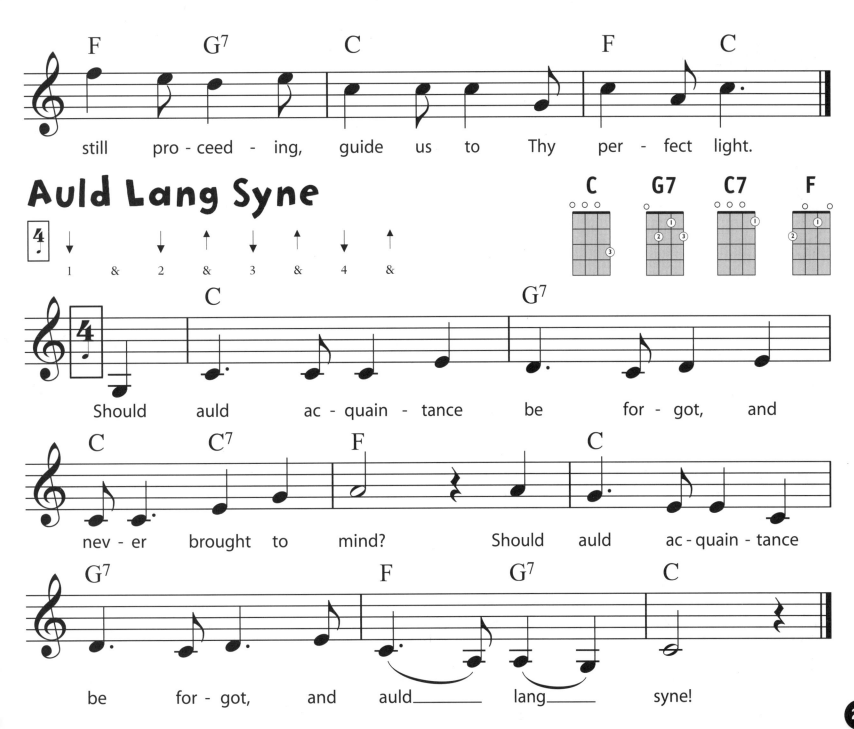

still pro-ceed-ing, guide us to Thy per-fect light.

Auld Lang Syne

Should auld ac-quain-tance be for-got, and

nev-er brought to mind? Should auld ac-quain-tance

be for-got, and auld___ lang___ syne!

My Bonnie Lies Over The Ocean

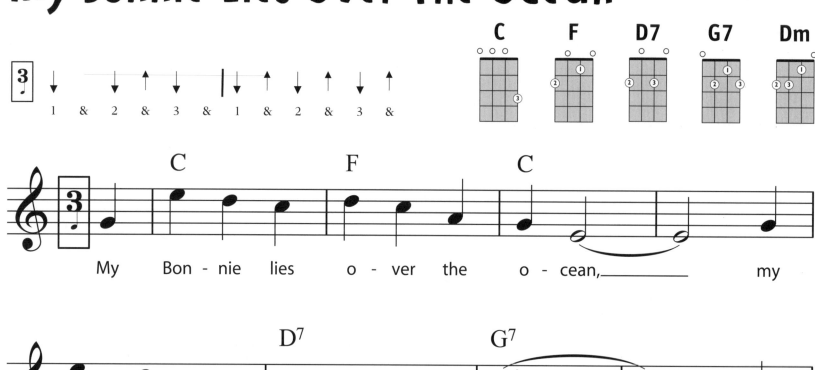

My Bon - nie lies o - ver the o - cean,_____ my

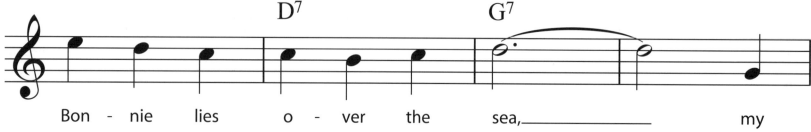

Bon - nie lies o - ver the sea,_____ my

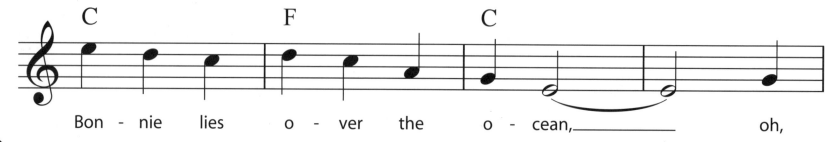

Bon - nie lies o - ver the o - cean,_____ oh,

Go, Tell It On The Mountain

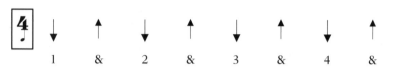

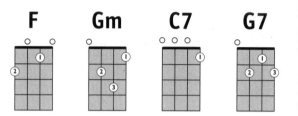

N.B. The '&'s should be swung.

Swung

Go, tell it on the moun - tain, o - ver___ the hills and

ev - 'ry - where,___ go, tell it on the moun - tain that

Je - sus Christ is born. The shep - herds feared and trem - bled when

Chord Library

F

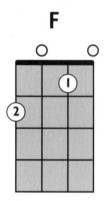

C7

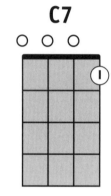

Gm

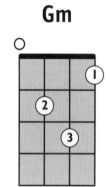

Dm

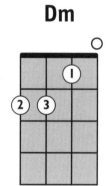

C

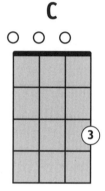

G7

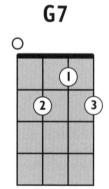

Am

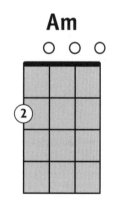

D7

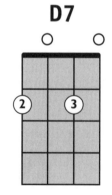

E7

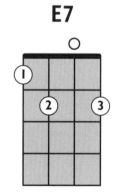